Lititz, Pa 17543

WHAT THE LIGHT WAS LIKE

WHAT THE LIGHT WAS LIKE

POEMS

LUCI SHAW

WORDFARM
LA PORTE, INDIANA

ALSO BY LUCI SHAW

POETRY

Polishing the Petoskey Stone
Writing the River
The Angles of Light
The Green Earth
Water Lines
Accompanied by Angels

NONFICTION

God in the Dark
Life Path: Personal & Spiritual Growth through Journal Writing
Water My Soul
The Crime of Living Cautiously

ANTHOLOGIES

Sightseers into Pilgrims
The Risk of Birth
A Widening Light

WITH MADELEINE L'ENGLE

WinterSong: Christmas Readings
Friends for the Journey
A Prayer Book for Spiritual Friends

FESTSCHRIFT

The Swiftly Tilting Worlds of Madeleine L'Engle: Essays in Her Honor

WordFarm
2010 Michigan Avenue
La Porte, IN 46350
www.wordfarm.net
info@wordfarm.net

Cover Image: Getty Images

Design: Andrew Craft

USA ISBN-13: 978-0-9743427-9-5
USA ISBN-10: 0-9743427-9-3
Printed in the United States of America
First Edition: 2006

Library of Congress Cataloging-in-Publication Data

Shaw, Luci.
What the light was like : poems / Luci Shaw.-- 1st ed.
p. cm.
ISBN-13: 978-0-9743427-9-5 (alk. paper)
ISBN-10: 0-9743427-9-3 (alk. paper)
I. Title.
PS3569.H384W47 2006
811′.54--dc22

2006004526

P 10 9 8 7 6 5 4 3 2 1
Y 12 11 10 09 08 07 06

ACKNOWLEDGMENTS

Christianity & Literature: "As iron on iron" and "Without regret"

Crux: "The grit on the track"

Episcopal Voice: "Sensing"

I Have Called You Friends (writings in honor of the Very Reverend Frank Griswold; Cowley Publications, 2006): "Crossing" and "Sensing"

Image: "Botticelli's *Madonna and Child, with Saints*"

Nimble Spirit (online poetry journal): "Deluge," "The grit on the track," "Into the blue," "Life drawing" and "Tenting, Burr Trail, Long Canyon, Escalante"

Radix: "Present"

Rock & Sling: "Sometimes God speaks in blue" and "Time travel"

Sojourners: "Tsunami"

StoneWork (Houghton College online literary magazine): "Botticelli's *Madonna and Child, with Saints*;" "Light gathering, January;" "Revival;" "Tenting, Burr Trail, Long Canyon, Escalante" and "The fixer-upper"

Weavings: "The simple dark"

The poem "Present" was reprinted in *Proclaiming the Scandal of the Cross,* edited by Mark D. Baker (Baker Academic, 2006).

for Margaret Smith

CONTENTS

FOREWORD

Back before e-mail became the preferred means of communication, I loved postcards. (I still do; they cost less than first-class "snail" mail, they oblige the writer to be concise, and they need to be written by hand, which seems so much less mechanical and more human than sending a message from a screen.)

Whenever I was in a museum or gallery, I would buy some favorite reproductions of paintings on postcards. Or in Istanbul or Vienna or London, I'd purchase postcard photographs of local scenery from a revolving rack on the street. I have cards that I've hoarded for years—so fond of them that I don't want to let them go, even to my closest friends. Sometimes they're the only reminder I have of a journey, or what a balmy Pacific island or a field of Welsh sheep or the turrets of an ancient castle in Scotland looked like. They refresh my imagination by waking my memory.

My friend Margaret Smith, herself a gifted poet and kindred spirit, would reciprocate whenever I sent her a card from, say, Iona, to describe the slant of late winter light on the Abbey or the brilliance of midday in the Colorado Rockies. She would let me know how powerful the light was in California or the Oregon Coast or Dublin. "What the light was like" became our antiphonal theme. Back and forth the cards came and went for years. Some of our word pictures ended up in poems. Images are like that; they tend to attach themselves to nouns and verbs and adjectives.

Now I live on the most northwestern tip of the U.S mainland, and in the winter our nights are long and our days are short. We get up in the dark and cherish the brief hours of daylight before night returns. Because of its scarcity, light has become a value, a necessity. You've heard of seasonal affective disorder. I have nine skylights in my house just to keep my sanity. Every day now (I'm writing in January), thanks to earlier sunrises and later dusks, we get a couple more minutes of light, a physical quality we have learned never to take for granted.

Inevitably, the subjects of photography and painting being what they are, the images include the bright and the dark, color and detail illuminated by light and highlighted by contrasting shadow—a kind of *chiaroscuro*. Light has a peculiar quality of transforming what it touches, like gold foil over wood. In Hebrew the word for *glory* has the sense of heaviness, as if light adds to the bulk of its significance. When I see the road that runs in front of my house and the bushes along the sidewalk touched with sunlight, even the black tarmac and the faded winter leaves look glorious.

The word *light* bursts into multiple meanings. Think of light's brightness, and its lightness as opposed to weight. To light a candle is to ignite it. The word also brings to mind the opposites that give it meaning by contrast—light and darkness, light and heaviness, to light and to extinguish.

But now, to hark back and hope forward. This book is for Margaret and for all the lights and shadows our lives have both been flooded with—the weights and buoyancies; the ignitions and insights; the landscapes, showings and scenes; and the celebrations of the senses in which the soul resonates with its context.

Poems try to do the same thing—they paint a picture and show the effects of light on the subject. I'm hoping that the pictures these poems print in your mind will be the kind of postcards you'll want to keep.

Luci Shaw
Bellingham, Washington
January 2006

Outside

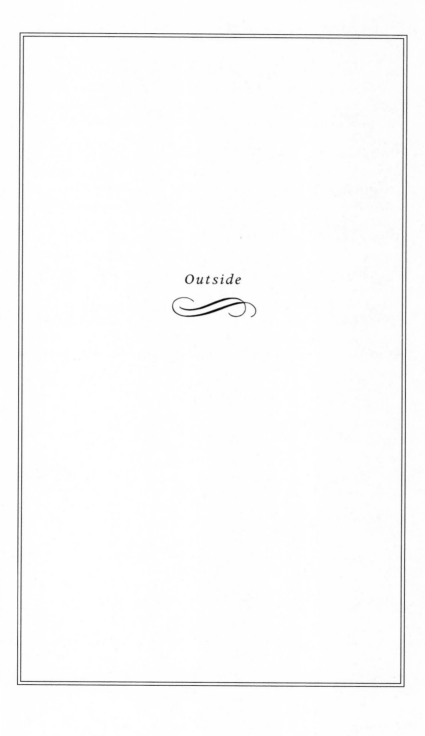

TENTING, BURR TRAIL, LONG CANYON, ESCALANTE

Even when I close my eyes, even later in
the tent, dreaming, I see banks and rivers running red.
My blood has drunk color from the stones as if
it were the meal I needed. I am ready to eat
any beauty—these vistas of stars, storms.
The mesas and vermillion cliffs. The light they magnify
into the canyon. The echoes, the distances.
The rocks carved with ancient knowledge.

But after vast valleys I am so ready for this
low notch in the gorge, the intimate cottonwoods
lifting their leafy skirts and blowing their small
soft kisses into my tent on the wasteland's
stringy breath. The spaces between the gusts are rich
with silence. I am ready to stay in this one place, sleep,
dream, breathe the grace of wind and earth that is
never too much, and more than I will ever need.

In this parchment land, the scribble
and blot of junipers and sagebrush—each crouched
separate, rooted in its own desert space—
spreads low to the sand, holding it down
the way the tent pegs anchor my tent, keep it
from blowing away. The way I want my words
to hold, growing maybe an inch a year,
grateful for the least glisten of dew.

SINGING BOWL

After we have doused the light,
a few howls, then the dog settles uneasily
to sleep.
                    Conversation dwindles
until there is no sound but a rattle
of dry wind against scree, like the stroking
of a rough animal pelt. At the foot of the cirque,
where the ice of ages melts down into
the forked river called Nooksack,* we are held
in the palm of a great hand. Through the tent flap
the stars overhead radiate from
the "hammered dome," what the ancients
called the firmament, but so pliant we want
to finger it, to pull it on, dusky, like a cap
against frost.
                    In its wide circle beyond
the tent floor the moraine begins its curve up—
a ring of mineral difficulty rising to
the glacier's shoulders, spun with rock. Caught
in this bowl, our hearts remind us of the way
grains of sand are whirled by wind and water
within concavities in the rock face
so that eons later the sandstone honeycombs
into a marvel of abstract art.
                                        We listen for
that rotary singing—the circular voice of the soul
ringing in our own souls, carving us.
The chime of our creation doubles back, a hum
of matter, a gong of a word spoken
before our birth, before the golden bowl

was broken, the silver cord snapped.
                                        The dog
begins again to chant his own song, pitched
to the moon rising like an orange over Shuksan.

* *The Nooksack Cirque lies in the lap between Mt. Shuksan and Mt. Baker, in the Cascade Mountains of Washington.*

THE SIMPLE DARK

Black birds slice their evening patterns—
long curves in the sky. Everything
is drawing down into shade.
But the dark, which is at first so simple
is not simple. Away from the farmhouse
with its slits of yellow, the monochrome
develops like a print in the chemical bath.

The unbroken velvet swims
with complications so subtle that
seeing and hearing must take their time
to know. The shadow purples,
the dusk intricate with crickets. The sky
infested with pricks of light.
My whole body an ear, an eye.

INTO THE BLUE, ALASKA

Strapped into the motorized mosquito by
the Tlingkit pilot, who, for $89 an hour, lifts us up
over Petersburg—its fishing boats, its smell
of halibut, its thousand circling gulls—we rise.

Below, the red buoys shrink and vanish
in the channel's burnished blue steel.
It's better than 3-D: there is sound and
this is life and my camera is hungry

to furnish my future with this drama. Beneath us,
in LeConte Fjord, the cakes of ice float like
crumbled Styrofoam in a bathtub. Soon, as we ascend,
layers of mountains begin to arrange themselves

in a contour map. We tilt over the glacier itself,
a sluggish, high river of dirty blue-white.
This old snowfield, drawn down to its destiny,
pleating itself as it turns, makes sounds like

thunder and rifle shots, surrenders, calves
violently, splits azure, loses itself in a clutter
of frozen gemstones large as buildings that plunge
into a bay of cobalt between the great unmoving knees

of rock. The whole fjord heaves with blue. And now
I have run out of film. My eye, my truer lens,
dyes my mind like a chemical with the color of sea
and sky. I am seeing these lines in blue ink.

MOVING

Little grass snake coiled in the sun
on my front step, you seem to me
an *objet d'art* carved from ebony and ivory.
I love your stillness, yet quick as winking,
when I shift, you unwind
over the edge, into invisibility
among the clumped astrancias.

Enchanted, I watch the garden sprinkler,
its bright fan of beads rising
and falling across the feathered grasses.
As though the arcing sun had lowered,
partner in a slow dance with water
at the turn of a tap. So easy, and
the ground is so grateful.

Ruby-throated hummer, glad not to be
anchored, not a stone bird, I extol
your tiny flexible claw, your articulated eyelid,
the way a wing works in air, your bright
volatility of spirit. Loving you, I am witness
to the sacrament of gesture. Your ballet
releases me into my own tentative dance.

AS IRON ON IRON

Walking this morning, I began to think
how everything wears its other down. How
this sidewalk smoothes my rubber soles.
How stomachs slick their food, waves
burnish shattered bottles to sea glass,
how a prevailing wind shapes trees
and bends them to its gusting will.
How calm weather soothes an impatient sea.

A panther, crated for the zoo, will pace
her pattern in her cage. Today my open window
carves the sunlight to a square that warms
the rug. God tools me like a strip of buckskin.
My silence wears your chatter like a suit;
your charity unravels my reproach. You
shape me, and I shape you, and all our kindred
work to shape us into who they wish we were.

GETTING ON BOARD

Sometime make time to step
into the boat just as it leaves the berth.
It's overcast, but listen—
water chuckles at the hull. Tackle slaps.
It is a child new from the birth canal,
ready to try the weather of the world,
to let the tide and its turbulence have
its way, or to resist, heaving its push
against the rudder.

Once out beyond
the breakwater, feel how deeply green
the bay is as it opens to the ocean. Continents
are waiting out there. Feel hope
as the clouds begin to go ragged
and dissolve. Marvel then at the sun,
nothing sly or shy about it, as if it has been
planning all morning to burst out.
It pours into the canvas
like heavy cream—so irresistible
it might swell the main and flesh out the jib
like food in a full belly.

When the gusts come, they seem
a series of conjunctions or irregular verbs
with more or less breath in them.
But the sun is a force,
a large noun in a language that needs
no translation. Now, ask yourself
why you felt so compelled to get

on board, to travel west, sailing
the earth's curve, the sun's path.

WITHOUT A SHADOW

The hill is steep and the walking slow,
and when I look back the road fades
to a pale nothing behind me.
Fog follows me, the drift of it
a clinging dampness that melts
the angled ghosts of cedar and fir.
Blotted out, their pungent scent intensifies.

The blurred red hydrant, the houses
below, the edge of the invisible shore,
are buried by a relentless creep
of skim milk, opaque, as if the view
has drained through the sink hole
of the lake (whose delicate
fog-blunted lapping rises to my ear).

Not exactly dark, but without shade,
the sharp purity of morning has been
diminished. I read somewhere that
"only full light reveals shadow."
Moving through fog, living
is a blindness, a yielding
of my layered ignorance to the mist.

A gleam on the tarmac
and indistinct tree shapes
angle across the road. A rumor of blue
begins to kiss its way through.

PRESENT

At light speed, God speed,
time collapses into *now*, so that
we may see Christ's wounds as
still bleeding, his torso,
that ready sponge, still
absorbing our vice, our toxic shame.

He is still being pierced
by every hateful nail
we hammer home. In this
Golgotha moment his body—
chalice for the dark weeping
of the whole world—brims,

spilling over as his lifeblood
drains. His dying into the earth
begins the great reversal—
as blood from a vein leaps
into the needle, so with his rising,
we surge into light.

THE BLUE EYEBALL

The grove, and this huge eucalyptus tree
leaning over me. In the clasp of two
saber-shaped leaves heaven looked like
the gaze of God peering through the eye of a needle.
The sky's air—intense as a rare bead of clear
cobalt sea-glass—God looked straight through,
through me, as though my transparency
were something he craved.

And then, rising from stillness, the air
began breathing, began rearranging
the leaves. Oh, they closed—God's eyelids.
Clouds arrived in their dark boats over
the waves of hills. My view of heaven
was shut. But then, in a thin wire
of lightning, he spoke into me the promise—
his view of me will not be held back
by clouds, two leaves, a forest.

PINK

Not a color I've wanted to wear—too
innocently girlish, and I'm not innocent,
not a girl. But today the gnarled cherry trees
along Alabama Street are decked out
like bridesmaids—garlands in their hair,
nosegays in their hands—extravagant,

finally the big spring wedding to splurge,
and hang the cost. Each really wants to be
the bride so she can toss her bouquet until,
unaccustomed, the gutters choke
with pink confetti that flies up and whirls
in the wake of cars going west,

flirting shamelessly with teenage boys on
the crosswalks. The pale twisters,
the drifts of petals, call out to me, "Let go;
it's OK to be giddy, enchanted, flighty,
intoxicated with color. Drive straight
to the mall and buy yourself a pink Tee."

Inside

BOTTICELLI'S *MADONNA AND CHILD, WITH SAINTS*

Jesus looking like a real baby, not
a bony homunculus, solemn and all-knowing.
The quill in the hand of his newly-minted mother
stretches toward the bottle of ink a beautiful boy saint
is holding out. He has waited for centuries for her
to write in a book the next words of her own Magnificat,
for the Gospel of St. Luke, and for us to sing in church.
Two other youths try to lower a crown onto her head.
It is too large for her, and they've held it there for so long,
but she seems bored with royalty, eyes only for
her son, and his for her. In her left hand, as she
supports the child, she holds a pomegranate
under his fingers for him to pluck, its red leather skin
peeled back to expose its packed rubies.
Centuries later the paint and the fruit are fresh
and tart as ever, glowing like blood cells.

I wonder about sound in the room—small talk among
the impossibly adolescent saints. Mary talking baby talk,
perhaps, or singing as if she has swallowed a linnet—
Mary with the pale green voice, nothing coloratura,
more like grapes glowing from a low trellis.
In the moist Italian twilight, a cricket is likely to be sawing
like the sawing of cedar boards in the workroom just outside
the painting's frame—Joseph laboring on a baby bed.
But there isn't a bird or an insect. There is just this lovely girl,
waking to motherhood, humming, content in this
moment in time, to be God's mother, to hold Jesus,
when he cries, to her leaking breast.

As Botticelli lifts with his skilled hand a fine brush
to add the next word to her song, we look with him
through the lens of his devotion into this ornate room.
He paints love pouring through her skin like light,
her eyes resting on the child as though
he is all there is, as though her knowing will never
be complete. Right from the beginning,
How can this be? circles her mind with its echo.

FERTILITY

How astonishing it is
when some floating sense of exaltation
or desperation sharpens into
a phrase that bursts, uninvited,
into consciousness,
a sudden siren in the valley.

Under my listening for words,
I stroke the waxy skin
of peppers at the market. I hear
scarlet, green, gold, and end up not taking home
anything but color.

The signal, searching,
reaches out and clasps another bright
shard of speech, a partner out of
thin air, who then welcome others
and arrange themselves in couplets or tercets,
even a quatrain, mating
orgasmically to reproduce with the intensity
and release of sex.
                                        And soon
this little jewel of a thing is born
and grows up to be a poem.

MANNA

They asked, and he brought quails,
and gave them food from heaven. Psalms 105:40

I'm not asking for quails for dinner
and, if they flew in my window, at mealtime,
in a torrent of wind, I would think
aggravation, not miracle.

Time is so multiple and fluid. If I lose a day
flying the Pacific and gain it back
returning, perhaps the prayer I offered
this morning at first light
was known and answered last week.

You never know what a simple request
will get you. So, no plea for birds
from heaven. Rather, I will commit myself
to this quotidian wilderness, watching for what
the wind may bring me next—
perhaps a minor wafer tasting like honey
that I can pick up with my fingers
and lay on my tongue to ease, for this day,
my hunger to know.

LIFE DRAWING

for Barry Moser

I've never posed naked
as a class analyzes my lights
and shades, the versions of flesh
variously translated as lines on paper.
The body not as I would like it—
sturdy bones and angled planes.
Instead, slackness and disproportion,
though that, too, is real
and worth the understanding.

This is how I think it would be
to have those easels circling, the artists,
charcoal in hand, studying my body
like a landscape. Their paper would become
my skin. I'd hear the soft sweep
of graphite and feel the Conte crayon
on newsprint—so intimate, the shape
massaged by glances and guesses. Eyes intent
on following the droop of breast, the curve
of thigh, the crescents of brow and jaw—
nipples and other shadows all yielding to
the multiple caress.

They'd work to get beyond surfaces,
to penetrate what lives
inside. To find some kind of essence—
the soul within the structure, taking
my body in their eyes and fingers
in a kind of lovemaking.
I the love object.

BREATH

When, in the cavern darkness, the child
first opened his mouth (even before
his eyes widened to see the supple world
his lungs had breathed into being),
could he have known that breathing
trumps seeing? Did he love the way air sighs
as it brushes in and out through flesh
to sustain the tiny heart's iambic beating,
tramping the crossroads of the brain
like donkey tracks, the blood dazzling and
invisible, the corpuscles skittering to the earlobes
and toenails? Did he have any idea it
would take all his breath to speak in stories
that would change the world?

MEMORY HOLDS

Imagine the first time the pentateuchal urgency arose—
to tie the high priest around the foot with a rope, so that fallen
he might be jerked back into the open from the hidden place
made more holy by fear of divine annihilation.

That dread—was it warranted? From here and now, extinction
seems impossible. Memory holds. Invisibility cancels itself,
being named. Even now, behind its blank scrim of cloud, I can trace
with one finger, on my car window, the outline of the shrouded
    mountain

glimpsed so often from the highway. The darkest secrets
are witnessed by their adjacent atoms, by precarious dust
and scattered, probing light. And by that searching eye
for whom night, distance and pseudonym provide no shield.

There can be no true solitude, no authentic escape,
no forgetting, even in death. After the corruptible body
has liquified, an image remains in God's mind.
And we remember.

SENSING

St. Paul's, Bellingham

A bloom like phosphorescence shines on
the newel posts at the ends of the pews. Is it the candles
standing on the altar, fat and white as milk,
with their heads on fire—vowels of light? Is it

the winter sun bleeding through stained glass
so that our faces begin to burn like lanterns?
Is it the air, with its brew of scents: varnished wood,
heat from the old radiators, and a whiff of consecrated oil?

There's the salt of old sweat, a profligacy of spice—
pungent distress and quandary and creed.
The seed of faith being sown again and again,
the fragrance of psalms, and their ancient verbal music.

The brassy cross in procession, an organ flourish,
and kneelers that creak when we slump down, confessing.
Gospel words from the aisle and the pulpit, the tread
of steps up to the altar, shriven souls inhaling,

hands and lips lifted for food and drink, the giving and taking
of ourselves—the commerce of heaven. Perhaps it's a kind
of incense just to be *this*—the prosaic body of God with peace
and grace passed among us, and a few crimson choir robes.

ANCHORED

Flushed as a newborn, my rebuilt left ankle
has become the most imperious of my body parts.
The joint sleeps recumbent while all the body's strength
creeps to this lower member, the way
a new mother focuses her days and nights
on someone other, and frail. Slung horizontally
in its cast, a papoose in its carrier, this patient
heals its way to immobility. I am all ankle—
dem bones dem bones dem living bones . . . de talus bone
connected to de calcaneous bone—and up to tibia

and fibula—a joint designed to flex, anchored rigid now
by five steel screws, like pegs to keep a tent stable
in the wind. Each bone with memories of
the old casual springing, cornering rush of speed,
forest paths flying beneath me, the easy change
of direction. My foot remembers all it has given away
for painlessness—the electric charge of impact as well as
the blue-black sallows of sprain and fracture, the slow
deposit of ache and spur, the flakes of bone and debris—
on the X-ray my surgeon deemed it all "garbage."

Forced now to be still, I'm jolted, aware of my uselessness.
Through the window I watch weeds fill the spaces,
overtake my garden. Face up on the couch, I pray to the skylight
and watch the prayer as it flies up through the glass. I have
the time to pray. It is a little Lent; a penitential wait, a surgery
of spirit, a listening in silence until the bones achieve
a structural solidity, grow into each other, prepare again
to bear weight. I am an anchorite, attentive to what

my ankle has to teach me. Through the incision this
dishonorable joint performs its delicate work of instruction.

ROUNDING

I ask each of the icons above my desk
a personal question: That nimbus around
your solemn head—is it gold beaten so air-thin
it's only a wisp of wafer, like the round
leaf of fiber floated onto our tongues
at the altar? A circle—in a wedding ring
it speaks for a union without flaw. But if
it gets worn, lost, broken, may it be mended?
And the moon, fat as a pearl, a grape, a wheel
of cheese—in two weeks gnawed away a bit more
every night, like a wheat cracker, by
the mice of heaven—by what mystery is it fleshed out
to roundness like the planets, the suns?

At Eucharist the priest holds high, in his thin
hands, a disc almost as big as a dinner plate.
He bends this little sun vertically in half
and half again; it cracks each time with a sound
that splits the sanctuary like a sharp arrow, and us
with it. We take this broken Son onto our tongues,
swallowed, into our gut. Eating, we are made whole,
as we join bodily the holy Circle of God.

MENDING

Here I am, a needle in time,
a sharpness glinting through some poor
torn paisley of fabric, pulling the swift nerve of my suture
behind me through invisibility, then flashing
back out, eager for the next stitch and the next,
a hopeful mending of what will never be
a seamless garment.

As the fabric of seasons shrinks,
shreds again—fibers of old cloth
wearing thin, needing to be rewoven—
my failed needle waits for a spool of fresh, glowing thread,
keeping itself steel bright and its point
quick and its eye open
for the next rip.

WHAT JAMES DIDN'T SAY ABOUT THE TONGUE

That it is almost prehensile, a pink
muscle manipulating morsels of fruit, of slander.
That you can feel it, right now, tensing
in your mouth as it scans the possibilities of tang.
That it probes with equal avidity the cavity left
where the filling fell out and the heart
of the olive—toying with its little flag of pimiento.
That it obsesses over the sharp edge
of a chipped tooth or a canker in the cheek.
That it is aggressive in the sinuous frenzy
of a kiss and athletic in its efforts to search beyond
the lips to nose, to chin, or narrow to a little
hovering snake head of pure investigation.
Restless, a blind, amphibious animal,
ceaselessly testing the limits of its porcelain cage,
cunning in shaping breath into word: half-truth
or proverb, benediction or blight.
As original as Eden. As unmanageable.

CROSSING

My right hand—
when I cross myself—
patterns me with Presence
—Father, Son,
and Holy Ghost—
here in my head, my heart
(where I need it most),
my left side and my right.
Thus crossed before the cross,
I am signed both with
death and life,
the intersection of
darkness with light.

But with that crossing
in whatever holy place,
my dexterous right hallows
its sinister fellow.
Through Grace
rather than competing,
the agile blesses
the awkward part,
the strong (the one
that feeds me when I'm eating)
exalts the weak.

At Eucharist, or at table
for any sustaining meal,
the food I manage with
my right hand also feeds

the part less able
on its own to spoon or speak
for its own needs.
So, here I kneel,
left hand cupped under right,
taking for both enough bread
for the journey,
for each enough strength
for the week.

Downside

TIME TRAVEL

So, it's not that I am driving east across Washington
towards Montana, but that the tires are unrolling
this serried map—moist, unhurried, neon green in May—
like a carpet, the landscape shifting away beneath me.
Wyoming is flattening itself under my wheels,

and endless South Dakota. Sprawling animal limbs of hills,
their tawny skin unfolding like velvet, the low sun
catching the nap along the ridges. The perception of standing still
and watching the light dissolve. Coming up, Minnesota
and a huge weather front. Ahead, a bow of colors

paints over a thunderous electric brow of cloud. As I drive
through its arc, a wire of lightning connects me to heaven.
What I want to say—these lights in the middle of the tunnel—
it is all here, all now, where I am and where I have been
and where tomorrow I will be. Suddenly, the deer.

In the shadow light our encounter seems momentous.
She stripes her signature of blood and fur along the car
and vanishes into the forest. To die? I cannot know. I'm off again
with a sheared-off side-view mirror and a flash of feral presence.
Signals show up everywhere.

STORM AT LA PUSH, OLYMPIC PENINSULA

At the reservation the cottage shivers
with wind. A huge front is breaking right
in front of us. The earth's edge is frayed,
barely buttressed from waves
by the skeletons of old trees
so carelessly thrown around,
their bones stacked and naked.
At middle distance, a trinity
of sea stacks and their brave,
tortured growth of firs.

By morning, they are just shadows,
ghosts behind the sheeting rain
moving across the view like smoke.
Even the gulls are blown backwards,
flighty as leaves, suspended in the power of air.
Walking, drenched after half an hour
of raking wind and rain, we stumble back
into shelter, gasping, hoping
for exorcism by strenuous weather.

The cabin window frames the world
as we wait it out, restless, unresolved.
About one-thirty the lights flicker, then
all the power goes. "It usually takes two
or three days," the clerk at the little general store
tells us as he rummages in the gloom
for candles and matches. The wind rises
and falls, a dramatic reading, the pauses between
heavy with omens. By late afternoon

an envelope of fog has opened its mouth
and swallowed us.

Daylight fades. You pick at your guitar,
the chords hesitating in the air.
Stitch by stitch my knitting
counts off the minutes before
dark folds us in its deep unknowing.

THE REDRESS

Your eyes are furtive, yet you wear
your gestures like a too-large shirt
bought for you by someone else
out of pity, because you were naked.
Nothing quite corresponds. Your hands flail,
movements too grandiose to match
your flat little soul. Even your smile
seems pasted on; the worry lines engraved
between your pastel brows betray you.

How if I were able to undress you, bind you
with fresh skin, smooth your unruly hair
and your feral shyness, hold you in to your
own self, the seamless flesh clasping
your bones, joints freed, feet beginning
to follow where your heart wants to go.
I am shopping for a dress that fits
and flows around you, a silky second skin
that will keep growing as you grow.

HOW TO RAISE FAULTLESS FLOWERS

My mother was a British gentlewoman
in an era of gloves and little hats with veils,
(I have her silver calling card case,
and the cards—her name engraved delicately,
black on ivory). She had such good taste it was hard
to please her. She was never wrong.
She arranged her mantlepiece symmetrically—
pale green candles and Derbyshire pottery.
The silver was polished, the piano always
tuned. The visiting grandchildren
made sticky fingerprints on her wallpaper,
spoke often without being spoken to
and put their elbows on the table.

My mother loved her English garden
immoderately—the roses all fragrant perfection,
the violets and primroses in their neat borders,
bright and genteel as their names.
Because of her conviction that it made
the roses redder, the foliage healthier,
she would creep out early into the street,
trowel in hand, before the world was up, to glimpse
her garden and collect the steaming piles left
by the milkman's horse. She trained her honeysuckle
to climb neatly up the wooden fence
and pruned the stragglers into submission
like unruly American children.

IN REVERSE

Turn it all backwards. Turn time.
Unravel the half-knit sweater in
the knitting bag. Remove the spilled
wine from the rug, return the color of dark cream
to its fibers and take them back and back
to the sheep's back before shearing.

I want my life over. To do it
the way that would give me who I want to be
now. To have again chances I didn't take,
and take them.

Make me innocent. Sluice me of
infractions. Give me soft
pink skin and a soul so fresh that
I may love my mother again.

IF I'M LUCKY

If I'm lucky, I'll get more sleep tonight.
Possibly there's enough bread left
and I won't have to shop. I'm hoping I'll get
the chapter written and the poem will come out
right. If I am lucky, the phone won't ring
all day and the computer will obey me
and not go blank like my mind does.
If all goes well, the slugs will drown blissfully
in their saucers of beer. Maybe the deer
won't eat the tulips. Perhaps it will rain
enough for the dwindled creek to run
again, sibilant, and then may the rain
stop tomorrow, leaving only a pleasing
liquid bubble and blur to thread the ravine.
If she is brave, my daughter will someday
find the self within herself. If I am blessed,
she will forgive me. If the meteorologist
is right, the dry muscle of cold wind will weaken
and again we'll swing the windows wide.

TOLERANCE

We think the virtue of tolerance
common enough to have become
an absolute, a necessity on our daily
shopping list. Sunday School Love
has become Accept. The maxim
Always Be Nice instructs us to ignore
iniquity. Eyes averted, we practice
the invisibility of the offence.

Like the cross, love may be weakened
through wear and age and such ubiquity
we hardly see it now for what it is,
hung high on the wall, or jeweled
around the rock star's neck. Yet,
precious as porcelain, love is bone strong.
Even chipped, it is still beautiful.
It glows through tolerance; like light,
it cannot hide. Remember,
love is made for something dire.

DELUGE

Think, if you were left behind.
A dead calm, sinister, then the first drops
and the river beginning to rise until
the tender tips of the grasses vanish, the wind,
the weeping trees, and days later
from the beach the wooden craft lifting,
buoyant with twinned animals. You listen
as the unlikely prophet and
his raucous offspring shout
goodbye to your doom and outrage.

Then the drenching gloom. Pewter waves
stretching to every horizon with only
a far shadow mountain left of terra firma,
brine climbing your chilled limbs as
your mingled roars and tears meet the sky's.
Maybe you thought *good fishing*
when it started. Now you're the dead fish,
or will be when you've quit treading water,
and water drowns out air and everything
is over. And under.

TSUNAMI

Two weeks on, and the planet is still
droning like struck metal. The low coastlines
shiver, waiting to be wiped away
like dust on a shelf.

On a flight the laptops deploy all around me,
played by virtuosos, but not
a single musical note. Birds do better;
the note of water dripping in a bucket after rain;
crystal clinked with a spoon to get
our attention. The drumming
of short-term thunder.

But nothing chimes like the great gong
at the heart of the globe, a seismic moan
circling out. The waters throb within us for
the next bell's tolling, when the ocean boils
and hurls itself abroad as one more
green speeding mountain.

THE GRIT ON THE TRACK

The ground is always there witnessing
how you walk. You need light to travel
a dark path, and you need to travel light.
Otherwise the shadow that turns out to be
a boulder or a root will trip you,
and your heavy pack will bear you down
into the hard anguish of gravel
that is more than your knees can bear.
Even roadside dust clings to your heels as if
God is in every crystal of sand.

Gravity and the possibility of falling
will keep you aware. In the twilight you
come home from walking the dog in the woods
with the walk still clinging to you—twigs
and the stain of berries on your soles.
Each clot of sludge from the forest floor
answers back—another footfall. *This is all*
my handwork, he is saying. *Stay with this mud,*
this humus. Every next mile you walk
will be a revelation.

WITHOUT WORDS

East Point Retreat House, Gloucester, Massachusetts

Look, I can't find the words for it.
All I have is this golden fullness
rising in my chest, flooding my throat
like a pool of honey. The scent of storm
will do it, too, or the white arc of the wave
that is just exploding in the shape of a bird
across the base of the sea rock. The knots
of brambles with their saffron leaves, shaking
in the wind. Their berries of blood on thorny stems.

Will none of it last? It shrinks
and blackens with time. The leaves fail
and the berries fall to the ground
and the sea flattens, silky and sad,
with no underthrust of tide, no belt of wind.

And now I am listening not for the words.
For a translation. For some meaning
to settle, in the still air, like dew.

Upside

CHRISTA'S APPLES

for my daughter-in-law

Driving to Christa's through the old part
of this scattered town, it seems the sky has spread
a layer of clear happiness over the streets
still damp from last night's rain. Something about the light
unclenches me—the radiant face of the woman
on the crosswalk, the suddenly pellucid sky
over the bay, the smell of sea as I swoop
up Magnolia Street, my car making all the green lights.

Along with the rain, most of the leaves on
sidewalk trees have left us, revealing apples
like so many rosy beads along the silky stripped wire
branches. Then, at Christa's, I see piled in a bowl
the windfall apples from the yard, bruised,
some a bit wormy, but all glowing as if lit from inside,
offering themselves for pies and sauces
so tangy they leave you wanting more, more.

I love the crisp word *apple*, with its hard
and soft sounds, and the way apples ripen
from blossom to green fruit, distilling the sum
of summer until they're ready to give
their crimson selves away, the way light
offers itself without measure, the way Christa
reverses the Fall, slicing herself out to us—
her own tart sweetness—without reserve.

DOCTOR'S OFFICE

for John, my son

Experimenting as a small boy,
you'd learned to make with your mouth
the sound a drop makes in a hollow well.
A champagne pop. A nutcracker.
In medical school you developed
a pan flute, bird calls. Your lips
could purse to a brassy trumpet.
Your favorite (still almost involuntary,
in moments of reflection), a cricket.

Distracting a panicky child, a patient
at the clinic, you ask—"Can you whistle inward?
Try it? OK, now, collect a spoon's worth of saliva
on your flattened tongue, and draw your breath in
sharply so it ripples the little lake of spit.
Practice, and you'll make a
true crickety sound."

You do it again—a thready chirrup.
Surely there's an insect in the office
repeating itself. With the reedy signal
in insect Morse—*No fear; I'm here*—fright
arcs away, wings snapping across the pasture.

DRAW ME

The stem leads down, past thorn,
past mud and darkness, to the root,

and thrusting upwards,
to the flower and fruit.

Through its blackened thread
the candlewicks draw wax into a glow.

Plumbing invites the water's
drainward flow.

The finger guides to its desired habitat
the nuptial ring.

Life winds its steel wire, coil by coil,
into a spring.

Curiosity may leave the beaten track
for some delicious, hidden place.

Night welcomes the risen moon
into a spacious embrace.

A verb's inevitably
attracted by a noun.

Follow the country road long enough,
you'll find the town.

REVIVAL

March. I am beginning
to anticipate a thaw. Early mornings
the earth, old unbeliever, is still crusted with frost
where the moles have nosed up their
cold castings, and the ground cover
in shadow under the cedars hasn't softened
for months, fogs layering their slow, complicated ice
around foliage and stem
night by night,

but as the light lengthens, preacher
of good news, evangelizing leaves and branches,
his large gestures beckon green
out of gray. Pinpricks of coral bursting
from the cotoneasters. A single bee
finding the white heather. Eager lemon-yellow
aconites glowing, low to the ground like
little uplifted faces. A crocus shooting up
a purple hand here, there, as I stand
on my doorstep, my own face drinking in heat
and light like a bud welcoming resurrection,
and my hand up, too, ready to sign on
for conversion.

THE FIXER-UPPER

Take the old house we just bought
on Jersey Street. Uninhabited for years, a century or more
of damp and wind, moss lying thick on the roof tiles,
walls inside exhibiting a bruised watercolor of mildew,

the footed bathtub with its scaled metal taps,
its resolute rust stain. The spaces between the studs
stuffed with yellowed newspapers and old
Bellingham politics. The floorboards, polished

by decades of stockinged feet, give a little
under our footsteps, though the place
is grounded in bedrock, the obstinate earth.
Brambles embrace the house's bleached siding

in slow armfuls. The ground under the apple tree,
rich with generations of rotten apple mush, feeds
the life cycles of worms. The old walnut in the yard,
a tree that each year spreads a little more shade, holds up

slanted panels of leaves to catch and hold
any light that comes. Like the windows, clouded
by cataracts of dust, waiting for clarity,
we welcome that light every morning it doesn't rain.

GOD SPEAKS IN BLUE

for Sophia

My friend hands me a gift
from overseas. "Here," she says.
"For you." The small packet rustles
with dry particles; through thin paper
my fingers feel the nubs. I thank her,

turning over the plain brown envelope.
There, from the other side, a photo—
the vivid, blunt cross of *Mecanopsis Betonicifolia,*
a Himalayan Blue Poppy—looks at me with
its gold eye, four azure petals blazing.

A blue to color a dream. The blue
of Mary's mantle according to Raphael.
The blue at the heart of a gas flame, within
an ice cave, on a cerulean door in a white wall
on Santorini, a kind of blue that

catches my heart ajar and blows it wide open.
Dry seeds and a picture, until next spring.
But, oh, if only I could be alive enough
to burn like this flower. If only
I could bloom as blue as this.

LIGHT GATHERING, JANUARY

Yesterday the sky began to drop small
handfuls of snow, randomly, like a fine
seed of hope being scattered onto the rooftops
to rumor a larger world. Or like pinches
of salt rubbed between bunched fingers
to season the season. Brightness gathers here,
there, anywhere—these crumbs of a white sky
fall and fall like so much mercy, hushed
and persistent, each crystal startled after
the long descent, a glistening prism that rides
down the window glass of the world
on the sled of its melting.

Today, this moment, the sun surprises us,
folding its congregation of light into
the half glass of water someone has left
on the windowsill, translating the white wood
and the pale wall into fans and feathers of color
so bright they're unearthly. A thaw is beginning,
and now I bless this afternoon for its golden drizzle,
drops of it hanging radiantly from the dogwood's
naked branches, as if everything, everything,
is suspended in their dazzling lenses,
the tears of the firmament caught
and held in strings of little worlds.

MOON SHINE

Don't fall asleep in the moonlight;
it will make you mad—
my mother's father's warning.
A doctor, Welsh, he was
a little mad himself, though not
from moonlight.

Some say the full moon
adds to the number of biting dogs,
traffic accidents, suicides
and other mischiefs. Moonstruck
lovers may be witched
into promises they cannot keep.

But I commend the glowing moons
that wash the fields with enough radiance
for farmers and spring sowing. That see
new babies conceived, and obedient tides rising
and falling in women and oceans.
That wash away flotsam, that restore beaches,
that allow kelp and barnacles
their six-hour breath.

I have slept often under the moon.
That wasn't what turned my hair white
or nudged my grandfather toward lunacy.
For those of us who love the slow benediction
of a ghost moon through a skylight,
or the bogey shadows on a night wall,
let us remember those gentle hours

when we have all lifted our faces to heaven,
wondering at its secondary light, our own
silvered features reflecting something
too pellucid and mysterious to be rational.

No telling what the young corn feels
as the moon pulls the green juice
up through the stem to the kernels
just beginning to fill with sweetness,
but I feel my own body shudder
with the fruit of light.

NEXT TO GODLINESS

As the Master swept out seven devils
from the Gospel habitation, so the best cleaners—
sturdy preachers of good news like our Rose—
have their way with houses. The rugs, without
demur, yield to the vacuum's vigor their dog hairs,
sand and stains. In the laundry room,
dirty clothes come clean. Rumpled underwear
and PJs resolve into neat piles. Shirts
lie meekly down under the steam iron to achieve
a sinless perfection—shame's creases erased.
The brass candlesticks, having accrued
slow months of tarnish, now relinquish it
to the polishing rags so that a gratified face
smiles back in love at their repentance. Rose
shows no mercy to spiders or their webs, revealed
by shafts of light and sternly dismissed.
Dust vanishes in filthy rags. Grease, that stubborn
outlaw, detaches itself, contrite, from
the stovetop. Little hills of crumbs humbly gather
in the dustpan like departing souls. Rose, prophetess
of clean, shows up to minister redemption in a time
of need, rebukes, cleanses, forgives, restores
and disappears to her own place. Or
to the house of the sinners down the street.

PETERSON'S PRIVY

Jan described it graphically, how,
when their old Montana outhouse was
torn down, it became an archeological dig.
Or maybe a plundered grave. Among
the rotting boards, a pack rat
was found to have woven into its
filmy nest—along with a red button, shreds
of tinfoil, a coffee spoon, a glove—
a photograph of Eugene's father in his youth.
His black-and-white likeness remained,
secret and benevolent, for close on
forty years, safe above the pit,
at the very mouth of that mini-hell.

O patron saint of the outhouse, O prophet
for generations of pack rats, O priest of
miscellany, O minister of penetrating effluvium,
O accidental sovereign, reclusive to
the point of anonymity, O icon of incarnation,
when your portrait was torn
from its shrine, how this sudden desecration
shattered the little rodent kingdom—
an Ascension into the cloud of unknowing.
All that was left was a pale, rectangular void.
This mystery is still whiskered in the scurried halls
of the Protectorate of the Pack Rats.

SMALL CHANGE

It doesn't grow on trees,
but in my daughter's garden it winks
small and silver from the money plant,
each translucent seed a miniature window that
opens up from the heart of a generous stem.

Once, in California, feeling a poverty of spirit,
I planted a sapling labeled "Silver Dollar,"
leaves round as coins, multiplying greenly
without effort or risk. It didn't buy me anything
but pleasure and a pair of backyard photos:
Eucalyptus 1, Eucalyptus 2, jade-tinted circles
held together by spider silk
with the spider herself poised in her house
of merchandise, guarding the dividends.

Today, in Bellingham, even the sidewalks gleam.
Small change glints from the creases
in the lady's mantle and the hostas after
the rain that falls, like grace, unmerited.
My pockets are full, spilling over.

WRONG TURN

I took a wrong turn the other day.
A mistake, but it led me to the shop where I found
the very thing I'd been searching for.

With my brother I opened a packet
of old letters from my mother and saw a side of her
that sweetened what had been deeply sour.

Later that day the radio sang a song from
a time when I was discovering love,
and folded me into itself again.

WITHOUT REGRET

The slug—how he melts
(the psalmist tells us) as he flows
over stones, painting
a trail of light
that leads me
nowhere I need to go.

The snake writes his way
through scrub, bruising no whisker
of fiber. Only a line like a finger
drawing on sand.
In spring an empty
silver sleeve shapes the air.

Glass has no memory. Drops
track down and vanish,
leaving no stain.
Every year winter shrivels, white
tissue paper in a flame.
No one minds.

ABOUT LUCI SHAW

Luci Shaw is a poet, essayist, teacher and retreat leader. Born in England in 1928, she has lived in Australia and Canada and (since 1950) in the United States. Author of a number of nonfiction books and eight volumes of poetry, she serves as Writer in Residence at Regent College in Vancouver, Canada. She also travels widely to speak and teach on topics such as poetry, journaling and the Christian imagination.

Her poems have appeared in *Weavings, Image, Books & Culture, The Christian Century, Rock & Sling, Radix, Crux, Stonework, Nimble Spirit* and other publications. Musical settings for several of her poems have been composed by Knut Nystedt, Alice Parker, Frederick Frahm and Allen Cline. Many of her poems have been anthologized.

She lives in Bellingham, Washington, with her husband John Hoyte. Her website (www.lucishaw.com) reflects some of her many interests, including wilderness camping, sailing, gardening and nature photography.